NOT YOUR MOTHER'S GOOSE

TOPHER GOGGIN

ILLUSTRATED BY RICK CUNNINGHAM

Aladdin

NEW ENERGY RULES FORCE ALADDIN TO OUTFIT HIS LAMP WITH A COMPACT FLUORESCENT GENIE.

The story of Aladdin is part of the famous Arabian Nights collection, along with such well-known tales as *Ali Baba and the 40-Minute Wait for a Technical Support Representative Who Doesn't Speak English* and *Sinbad the Stand-up Comedian*.

Aladdin starts off as a poor ne'er-do-well street urchin that spends his days annoying his fellow citizens, lying, and taking money out of other people's pockets. Basically, he's a U.S. Senator in a fez. Unfortunately, in Aladdin's world, this is not a very lucrative lifestyle.

Things take a surprising turn for the better, however, when Aladdin's friendly neighborhood evil sorcerer dupes him into retrieving an enchanted lamp from an ill-tempered magic cave. Along the way, Al runs into some minor issues with the cave's security system (which more or less tries to eat him), but he dinks and dodges his way to safety. He then tells the sorcerer "finders keepers" and holds on to the loot himself, ending the day plus-one in the lamp department. And still alive. Not bad.

Introduction
(a.k.a. Why You Definitely Need This Book)

If you are like many adults, you probably suffer from the misguided notion that fairy tales are no longer a top priority in your life. After all, the folks at the office probably aren't looking to debate the finer points of the *Princess and the Pea* with you over lunch. Plus, it's not like you've forgotten everything. You still know that when your 15-year-old son asks for your credit card so he can stream *Sleeping Booty* on Netflix, it would probably be wise to refuse. Isn't that good enough?

Sorry, but no. Here's the problem. You and I both know that it's only a matter of time before your annoying brother asks if you wouldn't mind taking care of his five-year-old twins for a couple weeks while he and his wife go to Tahiti and maybe never come back. And since you still owe him that fifteen grand he loaned you after the whole "incident" at the race track last summer, you're going to have to do it. (Otherwise your husband might find out.) Translation: You'd better learn some fairy tales. Soon.

Of course, it's not like you can go and major in Fairy Tale Studies at Ohio State. Only the football players can do that. That's why you need this book. Think of this as the *Cliffs Notes* of fairy tales and nursery rhymes. I have conducted years of painstaking research to bring you the most accurate and detailed reference possible.[1] In practically no time, you'll be an expert on witches, giants, wolves, mermaids, and naked emperors. From basics like the three dudes rub-a-dub-dubbing in the tub (the Butcher, the Baker, and Peyton Manning), all the way to obscure details like the name of the troll under the Three Billy Goats Gruff's bridge ("Steve"), you'll be pulling fairy tale trivia right out of your . . . glass. Uh, glass slippers, that is.

I'm gonna tell it to you straight, too. No more acting like the Little Red Hen is some sort of hero just because she managed to bake one loaf of bread without assistance. I mean, what kind of lazy ass has to ask for help baking bread in the first place? Same goes for the so-called Prince "Charming." Women drool over this guy like he's Brad Pitt,[2] but he's actually out two-timing Cinderella with Snow White, Sleeping Beauty, Taylor Swift . . . (Okay, maybe not Taylor–but that's only for fear that she'd write a song about him.)

And wait! If you order in the next 17 seconds, I'll throw in a special bonus. While doing my research, I discovered some newspaper stories and headlines involving our favorite fantasy characters. Just for you, I'm going to throw in those clippings—easily a $40 value–free of charge.

What are you waiting for? As far as I can tell, your only alternative is to take your brother's brats to *Kung Fu Panda 7*, and that's sure to end with you gouging out your eyeballs with the Milk Duds box. But that doesn't have to happen if you just read this book. Don't do it for me, do it for the sake of the children. Or the Milk Duds.

---

[1] By which I mean I Googled a few things and, when in doubt, relied on what I could remember from the appropriate Disney movie.
[2] As a side note, my aunt once tried to tell me, with a straight face, that I look like Brad Pitt. She might need a new optometrist.

Table of Contents

Aladdin . . . .
Bambi . . . .
Cinderella . . . .
Pinocchio . . . .
Hansel and Gretel . . . .
The Emperor's New Clothes . . . .
Peter Pan . . . .
John Henry . . . .
Rapunzel . . . .
Rumpelstiltskin . . . .
Jack and the Beanstalk . . . .
Snow White . . . .
Sleeping Beauty . . . .
The Little Red Hen . . . .
The Princess and the Pea . . . .
The Three Billy Goats Gruff . . . .
The Bremen Town Musicians . . . .
The Three Little Pigs . . . .
The Fox and the Hound 4
The Gingerbread Man 4
The Tortoise and the Hare 4
Little Red Riding Hood 4
Robin Hood 4
Stories You Don't Remember 4
Alice in Wonderland 5
Beauty and the Beast 5
The Jungle Book 5
Goldilocks and the Three Bears 5
Twitter 6
Facebook 6

He takes his new lamp home and, while trying to figure out where to screw in the light bulb, ends up rubbing the thing and causing a genie to magically appear. The wise-cracking magic man promptly informs Aladdin that he may have already won the chance to appear in a joke about a hard-of-hearing genie, and recommends that he wish for a 12-inch pianist. Aladdin, however, is more concerned with trying to get into the billowing pants of his favorite princess, and decides this would best be accomplished by wishing to become a handsome, elephant-riding prince. With a 12-inch pianist.

Of course, things are never quite so easy. While Aladdin is putting the moves on Her Highness and flying her all over on a magic carpet, the disgruntled evil sorcerer is still around. It's only a matter of time before he connects the new love-muffin prince in town with the little twerp that pinched his magic lamp a while back. The sorcerer steals the lamp back and puts the genie to work on some new wishes—wishes that do not exactly make Aladdin's well-being a high priority.

Having been around the block once or twice, Aladdin recognizes that the sorcerer's tactics were not entirely fair. He promptly turns the case over to law enforcement, knowing that the resources of the local police and district attorney will surely be more than adequate to redress the injustices committed by a powerful sorcerer with a genie at his disposal.

Admittedly, some of your less respected editions of this story have Aladdin prevailing over the sorcerer by other means. These methods include placing some wishes with a second backup genie (FYI, FEMA recommends all Americans keep a backup genie in their disaster preparedness kit), and/or convincing the sorcerer to wish to become a genie himself and then imprisoning him in his own lamp. Take your pick.

IKEA 2-for-1 Tuffet Sale a Surprising Flop

Van Winkle Patents "Snooze" Button

Bambi

A mother deer gives birth to a fawn, a MALE fawn, and names him Bambi. With an 'i.' Worst. Mother. Ever.

Unaware that he has been given a chick's name, Bambi grows up in the forest with a variety of other comically-named animals, including a rabbit named Thumper, a skunk named Flower, a wise-cracking giraffe named Biff, etc. They have many adventures together, frolicking in the meadow, sliding around on frozen ponds, and getting the f--- out of Dodge whenever Elmer Fudd shows up trying to shoot them.

Their story is just cruising along, upbeat, lighthearted—a completely joyous tale. Then, well . . . um . . . yeah. In possibly the most tear-jerking movie scene of all time, Elmer Fudd returns, and in a depraved act of heartless savagery, shoots Old Yeller. And Bambi's mom.

The story takes a sharp thematic turn at this point, transitioning from a little kid's movie into some sort of *Nature* special on animal reproduction. We've got critters pairing off and mounting each other left and right. Soon, despite their vow to never get "twitterpated" in love, even Bambi's friends succumb to their supercharged hormones. This includes the famous scene where, having acquired a girlfriend, a horny Thumper heads off to thump her.

Finding himself as the last single guy in a group of married friends, Bambi's first instinct is to go buy himself a Ferrari. Things change, however, when he runs into his childhood friend Faline, who is now smokin' hot. They quickly become an item.

It doesn't take long for the whole relationship thing to turn into quite the pain in the ass for Bambi. First he has to fight off a beefcake buck named Ronno that also has a thing for Faline. Somehow Bambi actually wins this battle. (You know if you were betting on a pay-per-view fight in Las Vegas featuring someone named "Bambi" vs. someone named "Ronno," you're plunking your cash down on "Bambi." Riiiiiight.) Once he dumps Ronno off a cliff, Bambi next has to rescue Faline from a forest fire, getting himself shot in the process. Bambi, dude, this girl is trouble. Cut her loose, man. In the end, though, all is well, as Faline and the Bambster escape, have twins, and apparently all live happily every after.

So, let's just summarize here: We've got forest fires, gunshot wounds, a dead mother, and animals humping and popping out kids all over the place. Movie rating: G. Clearly, putting a talking skunk in your story will fix anything.

A TOUGH CHOICE FOR TED

Little Red Riding Hood Inks Movie Deal

Back in the news once again, Little Red Riding Hood's attempts to extend her fifteen minutes of fame continued yesterday, as the ubiquitous damsel-in-distress announced that she has signed a movie deal. Little Red, who just last month tried to resurrect her stardom by releasing a hip-hop record titled "Lil Red in Da' Hood (featuring Bo Peep with Ol' Motha' Hubbard)," confirmed through her publicist that she has signed on to co-star with Sylvester Stallone in the upcoming direct-to-DVD release of *Rocky VI: Assisted Living*.

Little Red will play herself in the film, coaxing a 79-year-old Rocky to leave his walker behind and return to settle a score with a scoundrel he catches taking an unauthorized second dessert from his retirement home's dining room. The tension heightens when the brawl is delayed by a bingo game that runs long.

The movie is the latest in a series of attention grabs for Little Red. Her time in Hollywood has been riddled by tabloid appearances, including a drunk driving arrest in Beverly Hills where she was sentenced to 45 minutes of looking at a picture of a jail. With a song, horrible movie, and arrest already under her belt, commentators note that she is just one link away from the fabled D-List Grand Slam, needing only a clandestine sex tape with Jack Be Nimble to complete the set.

Pumpkineaters to Divorce

Another seemingly rock-solid couple appears to have fallen by the wayside, as Peter Peter Pumpkineater's wife Lois confirmed this week that she has filed for divorce. Though the news came as a shock to outsiders, online commentators were quick to blame the break-up on the emotional wear and tear caused by Mr. Pumpkineater's serial womanizing. In fact, *BuzzFeed* says it has already spoken to at least seventeen women who claim to have received explicit pics of Peter Peter's Peter.

Lois attempted to put an end to the rumors, telling reporters yesterday that, "The truth is, I've just always hated pumpkins." She refused, however, to comment on reports that she was recently photographed canoodling with her personal trainer, Buck Buck Pumpkinssuck.

With no children between them, the proceedings will primarily focus on the division of the Pumpkineaters' property. That includes their 1997 Winnebago Pumpkin Shell that legal experts say will probably just be made into a pie and sliced up.

Cinderella

In yet another example of the perils of divorce, Cinderella's father gets remarried, giving Cindy not only a new stepmom, but also two complimentary stepsisters thrown in for free. These stepsisters are complete bitches, but on the bright side, they're also totally ugly.

Along with their mother, they pretty much turn Cinderella into their personal butler, just without the spiffy uniform.

One day, everyone gets excited when word goes out that the hometown prince is holding a ball, including a contest featuring a top prize of becoming the prince's wife. (Also, the runner-up will get a nice set of steak knives.) Since every eligible woman in the kingdom is invited, Cinderella foolishly figures that she will actually get to go. Ha ha ha. Her stepmom and stepsisters instead decide that this would be the perfect weekend for Cinderella to wallpaper the living room, sweep the chimney, and clean the gutters, so she ain't going anywhere.

Cinderella holds things together for a while, but as she puts away the carpet shampooer and gets ready to start defrosting the freezer, she finally bursts into tears. No sooner has she started to gush like Old Faithful when **SHAZAM** a boisterous and excessively cheery woman appears out of nowhere to shower Cinderella with unexpected gifts. So this was either her Fairy Godmother, or maybe Oprah. Unclear.

The next thing Cinderella knows, she's dressed for the red carpet and riding off to the ball in one of those giant Miracle-Gro pumpkins that has turned into a carriage. As Cinderella departs, the Fairy Godmother makes a comment about a curfew or getting her parking validated or something like that, but, you know, whatever.

Things go quite well at the ball. The prince is enchanted by Cinderella's version of the Hokey Pokey and the Chicken Dance, and by the time the DJ spins the Macarena, he's head over heels in love. But right when he's about to order a ring and book the honeymoon in the Maldives, the clock strikes twelve, and Cinderella suddenly sprints out the door like someone just tweeted that Ryan Gosling was spotted in town. Her re-gourdified pumpkin carriage crashes sidelong into a bridge abutment, and the abandoned prince spends the rest of the night inconsolably moping in the corner like a five-year-old having a meltdown at his own birthday party.

The next morning, as the prince is helping his servants scrub the vomit off the ballroom

floor, he notices that his mystery maiden has left behind one of her glass slippers. A clue. He immediately enlists the help of O.J. Simpson to help him find the girl, hoping to draw on O.J.'s extensive experience searching for the "real killers." They take off on a cross-country search to identify the girl by having everyone with two X chromosomes try on the slipper. This begs the question: How small are Cinderella's feet that nobody else can fit in this slipper? Do the rest of the ladies in this kingdom wear clown shoes?

Regardless, you know the rest. Once Cinderella escapes from being locked in the broom-closet by her stepsisters, her foot slides in perfectly. (She also has the other slipper, but she could have just bought that on eBay.) Since the Prince's motto is apparently "If the shoe fits, marry it," he and Cinderella decide to take the pumpkin straight to Vegas to get hitched. As soon as she finishes re-roofing the shed.

Big Bad Wolf Grants Dying Boy's Wish By Eating Dr. Phil

Little Timmy Appleby may be terminally ill, but that couldn't keep him from having the day of his life yesterday, watching from the front row as the Big Bad Wolf devoured TV personality Dr. Phil McGraw in front of a live studio audience.

The thrilling encounter was set up after Timmy's parents told officials at the Make-A-Wish Foundation about their son's sickness. "He's always loved the Big Bad Wolf," Timmy's father, Duane, told reporters while fighting back tears. "To think that wolf would eat someone just for my little boy, it's unbelievable."

"At first I was going to have him eat Mr. McMacken, my English teacher," the adorable 13-year-old said afterward. "But then one day I walked into the kitchen and my mom was watching that dumb ass Dr. Phil. I knew right then it had to be him."

The experience was bittersweet for Timmy's mother, Lucy, who now will have to flip the channel over to Jerry Springer while she finishes her daily Thighmaster workout. "I know I'm going to miss Dr. Phil telling me to 'Get Real!'" she said. "But to see the smile on my little boy's face when the wolf was gnawing the last few bits of meat off those thigh bones, that was just priceless." Meanwhile, Dr. Phil's wife, Mrs. Phil, said she had mixed feelings about the project, but that was just because she missed out on the chance to see it when she incorrectly programmed her DVR and recorded the Premium Pots-N-Pans Hour on the Home Shopping Network instead.

Pied Piper Files Lawsuit Against Orkin

Citing trademark infringement and unfair business practices, exterminator Pat Peters of Pied Piper Pest Protection filed a complaint against the Orkin Company in Hamelin Circuit Court yesterday. Peters' paperwork postulates that Orkin is presently pilfering his patented pied piping procedure and purveying it for a pretty penny. Per Peters, Orkin personnel appeared to be purchasing piccolos and procuring pan flutes for the program. As you probably predicted, Plaintiff Peters' preferred pecuniary punishment is punitive damages.

Gingerbread Man to Host Fundraiser

A long-time local celebrity and philanthropist, the Gingerbread Man announced yesterday that he will host a fundraiser next month to fund prosthetic limbs for local amputees. "Helping amputees is a cause near and dear to my heart—for obvious reasons," he wrote in an Instagram post. "Nearly every member of my family has lost an arm, leg, or head along the way, and I am very excited to have an opportunity to give back."

He went on to indicate that no decision has been made yet as to what kind of fundraiser will be held, but admitted it's safe to assume that it won't be a bake sale.

PINOCCHIO

An Italian woodcutter named Geppetto builds himself a life-sized puppet called Pinocchio, then wishes that it would turn into a real boy. (Italy must have some weird adoption laws.) No sooner does he say this than a fairy drops by and brings the puppet to life. Well, almost. She lets him move around and think and such, but neglects to make him, how shall I put this gently, not wood. Instead, she cuts Pinocchio a deal. Be a good kid—unselfish, honest, occasionally mow the yard, etc.—and *then* she'll turn him into a real boy.

This whole "just behave yourself" experiment is not exactly what you would call a glowing success. Pinocchio promptly runs away from home, joins a puppet show, starts shooting pool, tries to sneak off to Pleasure Island, and invests Geppetto's life savings in the company that invented the ShamWow. Also, thanks to a little trick contained in the fairy-fine-print, his schnozz turns into your Uncle Larry's and grows every time he lies, which turns out to be frequently. (In fact, dork physicists and philosophers have wondered what would happen if Pinocchio ever said, "My nose is about to grow." Ponder on that one for a while. Especially if you have easy access to hallucinogenic drugs.)

Pinocchio's shenanigans prove to be no small

headache for his father. The trouble finally comes to a head when Geppetto, like so many frustrated parents these days, goes out to sea in search of his piece-of-crap kid and ends up getting swallowed by a whale. Pinocchio then goes looking for Geppetto—probably just hoping to borrow some cash or something—and gets himself swallowed by Shamu as well.

Somehow this all leads to Pinocchio's finest hour. Inside the whale, Puppet Boy makes like any good juvenile delinquent and immediately starts lighting shit on fire. The belly-blaze causes the whale to sneeze, and the next thing you know, Geppetto and Pinocchio are spewed forth onto the beach in a massive pile of ashes and whale snot.

At this point the fairy reappears and, seeing what's happened, is so impressed with Pinocchio's bravery and selflessness that she decides that he has finally earned the opportunity to become a real boy. (Either that or she realizes that it's going to be way too expensive to keep carrying him on her insurance coverage and decides she'd better just cut him the hell loose.) She grits her teeth, closes her eyes, and reluctantly utters the magic real-boy-making spell. ("Abracada-BRO," perhaps?) And then wishes upon a star that he never gets a job at a fireworks store.

Hansel and Gretel

If times are tough in your family of four, you might consider a variety of solutions: store-brand foods, carpooling, shorter showers, taking your kids out in the woods and leaving them, etc.

In this particular story, a woodsman and his new trophy wife opt for door number four. Alas, Mr. and Mrs. Lumberjack are not about to win any awards for subtle planning. While some children have to worry about accidentally walking in on their dad boinking the new wife, Hansel and Gretel instead wander in on their folks planning to abandon them in the forest.

Rather than make a quick call to Social Services, however, Hansel spends his last few hours loading up his pockets with white rocks. When the parents then lead the kids off into the woods, Hansel calmly dribbles a (completely unnoticed) rock trail behind them, which he and his sister later follow straight back to their house under the moonlight.

In a shocker, they don't get a terribly warm welcome upon their return. Before long, the woodsman's wife is again plotting to fix her problems by abandoning the kiddos out in the middle of nowhere. Unable to get to his rocks, this time Hansel is forced to lay down a trail of bread crumbs while he and Gretel are being led off into oblivion. This admittedly is not a horrible idea—definitely brighter than dropping, say, a trail of ice cubes. In the end it doesn't work, though, as birds eat the crumbs and destroy the kids' directions home.

Now stranded for real, Hansel and Gretel wander around for a few days until they stumble onto one of your more common sights deep in the forest, a house made entirely out of candy. Logically, they start eating it. This doesn't sit well with the homeowner, who turns out to be a terrifying old witch. The witch, who is nearly blind, promises the kids "real food" (probably drywall) and soft beds to lure them inside, where her real plan is to pork them up and eat them. Cause there's nothing like a delicious German child when you live in a house made entirely of candy.

The witch forces Gretel to be her slave and locks Hansel in a cage for feeding. Despite some tricks by Hansel to convince her that he is still skinny, the witch eventually loses her patience and orders Gretel to fire up the oven. Then, as Gretel preheats to 400°, the witch decides she would also like some Gretel Gruel for an appetizer. She slyly tells Gretel to lean into the oven "to see if it's hot enough." Gretel is no idiot, though. She responds with the famous "Oh, I Don't Understand What You Mean, How About *You* Get Into the Oven and Show Me How" Trick, which somehow totally works. Gretel slams the oven door shut—crisis averted.

Prior to getting the hell out of there, Hansel and Gretel prudently scope out the house, discovering that the witch's love of candy was closely rivaled by her propensity to hoard valuable jewels. The kids loot the place and take off for home, which they now somehow know how to locate. (Maybe the blind witch also owned a lot of maps.) When they get there, they learn that their bitchy stepmother has conveniently croaked, and once they ship the witch's jewelry off to Cash4Gold, the kids and the woodsman are pretty much set for life. Now somebody just needs to call Ellen DeGeneres.

Confused Kid's Version of "I'm a Little Pee Tot" Kills at Preschool Talent Show

The Emperor's New Clothes

An old-time emperor with a flair for fashion receives a visit from a couple of supposed "tailors." They inform him that they can update his wardrobe with clothes made of an extra-special fabric (I'm thinking polyester) that is so light it can hardly even be felt. Furthermore, this material they will weave is so incredible that it cannot be seen by people who are stupid, incompetent, or related to anyone who has ever worked at the Gap.

This grabs the emperor's attention. These clothes would not only put him on the cutting edge of fashion, but would instantly allow him to know which of his subjects are moronic idiots. He immediately places an order. The tailors don't exactly offer their product for five easy payments of $29.95, though, so the emperor has to fork over piles of gold, along with looms, thread, and some of those "Inspected by #47" slips to put in the pockets.

The swindlers promptly go to "work," putting on an Oscar-worthy performance of measurement-taking, loom-operating, seam-altering shenanigans. When they tell the emperor it's time to try on the finished product, he is stunned and dismayed to discover that *he* can't see the fabric, either.

The emperor, of course, is not about to own up to this fact, since doing so would require acknowledging that he is a complete dufus. Instead, he chooses the obvious alternative, scheduling a parade in his own honor to show off the new duds. Word goes out far and wide, and crowds assemble to see their esteemed leader in his updated wardrobe.

As parade time arrives, the tailors pretend to help the emperor don the non-existent clothes. He proudly strides naked through town in front of the throng of parade-goers (not to be confused with a "thong" of parade-goers, though that might be interesting, too). Having been informed that the unwashed masses will not be able to see anything, the viewers loudly heap pretend praise on the robes they too cannot see. With cheers like "what vibrant colors," "quite the exquisite train," and "such delicate embroidery," you'd have figured the emperor was the secret love child of Lady Gaga and Liberace (ask your parents, kids).

But just as the emperor is visualizing himself on the cover of *Vanity Fair*, dammit if some pipsqueak (who must not have gotten the whole stupidity memo) doesn't come and ruin the fun. The kid pipes up and says, "Dude, he hasn't got any clothes on." The crowd realizes that the boy is right, and that it's their naked emperor who is the buffoon here. This sadly is the end of the story, which concludes before we get coverage of the emperor's apology press conference afterwards. Just hope for a full-length podium.

Battle Rages Over Frosty's Remains

The relatives of baseball legend Ted Williams may have seemed crazy years ago when they were fighting about whether to put Ted's head into a cryogenic freezer. Their lunacy, however, pales in comparison to the current state of Frosty the Snowman's family, which continues to clash over what should be done with Frosty's remains after his untimely melting earlier this year.

When the five-day forecast made it clear that Frosty was not long for this world, his brother, Chilly the Ice-Carved Swan, placed a bucket at Frosty's feet to collect the drippings. Those droplets are now sloshing around next to a tub of cottage cheese in Chilly's refrigerator, much to the dismay of Frosty's mother, Gladys. (Gladys became even more distraught upon learning that Chilly's maid might have used the bucket while mopping the kitchen floor, meaning that Frosty is now sporting the fresh scent of Pine-Sol and technically may be a half-brother of Mr. Clean.)

Frosty's mother wants to take custody of the water and give it a proper disposal by flushing it down a toilet. "My son doesn't belong in a fridge, he belongs in a septic tank," she declared. Chilly, on the other hand, insists Frosty would have wanted to be preserved in case he could be re-animated for another frolic through town. Chilly believes that technology will soon exist that would allow Frosty to be taken to a local ski resort and misted through the snowmaking equipment, reforming him into flakes that could then be rolled and repacked.

Nursing Home Staff Catches Old King Cole in Scandalous Tryst in Old Mother Hubbard's Cupboard

Peter Pan

For this story we head to Neverland (the island, not Michael Jackson's house), a place where nobody has to grow up. It's a bit like playing for the Cincinnati Bengals. Our hero today is a young man named Peter Pan, the self-appointed leader of the "Lost Boys," a group that spends most of its time trying to outwit the neighborhood group of pirates. The pirates are led by Captain Hook, who frankly is a bit of an ass, though I suppose he might be perkier if Peter hadn't chopped off his hand and fed it to a crocodile. On the plus side, the Captain does have some snappy red outfits.

Our saga begins with Peter visiting London, where he meets up with three siblings named Wendy, Wendy's Brother, and The Other One. Peter teaches them how to fly, which involves sprinkling yourself with pixie dust and then thinking of a happy thought like not having a root canal. Plus paying $25 for your first bag and $35 for each additional bag.

Once they master their aviation lessons, Peter flies the group back to Neverland, where a love triangle develops between Peter, Wendy, and a fairy named Tinkerbell. In a rather aggressive step, Tinkerbell attempts to break up any budding Peter/Wendy romance by trying to kill Wendy. Thankfully, though, in addition to being unnecessarily jealous, Tinkerbell the Assassin is also totally incompetent. No worries. We've got a group of Indians hanging around the island as well, along with a shipwrecked guy in a bucket hat named Gilligan. Or something like that.

Over time, mass shenanigans ensue from the Lost Boys, pirates, and everyone else around. Captain Hook eventually kidnaps the children and comes up with a plan to make them walk the plank and kill Peter with a bomb. This plan, uh, doesn't work. Tinkerbell apparently moonlighted on the bomb squad back in the day, and in a rare moment of aptitude, takes care of all defusing-related issues. Peter frees the children prior to any plank walking, then out-duels Captain Hook and sends him prancing off in his tights with the crocodile in hot pursuit.

By this point, Wendy and her brothers have had just about enough fun and are ready to take Peter back to England to grow up. Peter decides to bring the entire posse of Lost Boys along, and has Tinkerbell bust out a three-kilo brick of pixie dust so he can fly the whole damn pirate ship back to London. Unfortunately, when they land at Heathrow, their gate is still occupied by a flying America's Cup yacht bound for Auckland. Unable to park, Peter makes the siblings jump off the ship on the run and turns tail back to Neverland with the Lost Boys in tow. They are still waiting for their luggage today. At least they won't have outgrown their clothes.

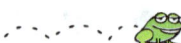

Not So "Little" Tommy Tucker Now Little Once Again:

Cuts Carbs and Drops 125 Pounds on Atkins Diet

White bread and butter may be delicious, but if you're looking to maintain that slim and trim figure, you might want to shut it down after your third or fourth loaf of the day. That's the word from famed vocalist "Little" Tommy Tucker, who watched his weight balloon to 315 pounds during his Wonderbread-sponsored *Toast of the Town Tour* last year. But that has all changed, as Tucker's publicist announced today that Tommy has ditched the carbs entirely and dropped 125 pounds on the Atkins Diet.

"It's all protein now," she said, noting that Tucker is also doing P90X, Zumba, CrossFit, Jazzercise, Sweatin' to the Oldies with Richard Simmons, and that PBS show with the old lady in a tutu who sits in a folding chair. No word yet on how he plans to update his trademark song, however, as nothing much seems to rhyme with cauliflower.

PETA to Protest "Popping" of Weasels

Old King Cole Receives Medical Marijuana Card

After years of dodging the drug dogs and hiding out on Willie Nelson's tour bus, Old King Cole can finally call for his pipe and his bowl without fear of prosecution. Citing chronic headaches from the stress of ruling wherever the hell he's king, Cole received his medical marijuana certification from the state yesterday.

"A merry old soul is me," the king told reporters as he strolled back from his mailbox with the long-awaited envelope. He then pulled a gigantic spliff out from under his crown and ordered his Fiddlers Three to chuck their violins in the royal dumpster and go get some sitars so he could space out on the throne.

Hare, Tortoise Selected in NFL Draft

A year after their famous road race, two local athletes are on their way to the professional football ranks, as both the Tortoise and the Hare were selected in the NFL Draft in New York over the weekend.

Previously ranked #11 overall by ESPN Draft Guru Mel Kiper, Jr., concerns about work ethic caused the speedy Hare to plummet to the late second round before being selected by the Tennessee Titans.

Meanwhile, the Detroit Lions stunned experts with their selection of the Tortoise in round four. Though initially seen by some analysts as a possible special teams contributor, the Tortoise's stock cratered after a poor performance at the league scouting combine that included a 40-yard dash time of 5.41 . . . hours. If history is any indicator, however, the Tortoise should still be one of the faster players on the Lions' roster.

JOHN HENRY

Apparently this John Henry guy might be real. (Source: The Internet.) Real or legendary, we're talking about a big, strong dude that decides it would be fun to make a living by blasting railroad tunnels through mountains. With a hammer. (If only he lived in the era of Wile E. Coyote, he'd know it's much easier to just paint what appears to be a tunnel entrance on the side of the mountain and then watch the Road Runner charge right through it.)

As the strongest, buffest guy around, Big John's popularity quickly shoots through the roof. But before he can buy a motorcycle and start cruising for chicks, some jackass has to come along and introduce a steam-powered drill that does the job instead. (It's kind of like when the guys from IBM showed up with a "computer" the size of semi-truck and acted impressed that it could play *Jeopardy*.)

Anyway, it appears that these drills might be just a tad bit more efficient than having guys tink-tink-tink with their hammers until they've blasted a hole through an f'ing mountain. That means all the tink-tink-tinkers will be out of their jobs, and John doesn't like that. After a solid brainstorming session, he concludes that he can personally solve the problem by setting up a one-on-one match between himself and the drill, with the winner getting absolutely nothing. Good call, John.

The ensuing battle is a legendary matchup, the mighty man hammering side-by-side with the machine, complete with Brent Musburger announcing on television (and rooting for the machine). Bing. Bang. Tink. Tunk. Finally, in a photo finish, Big John pulls out a heroic victory for all of humanity. And then he croaks. Drops dead. Right there on the spot. Oops. Have a nice day.

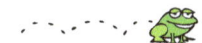

Rapunzel

Listen, I'm not saying that some people overreact or anything, but try this on for size. A husband gets caught by the kooky neighbor gal while he is committing the treasonous crime of stealing . . . her radishes. The lady's response? Threaten to kill the guy and his pregnant wife unless they fork over their new kid when she is born. Huh? If I ever got tricked into growing radishes and someone else was so kind as to come and steal them, I'd give that person a reward.

Regardless, the crazy woman gets the man to agree to this, picks up baby Rapunzel from the birthing ward, and does what any normal person would do in this situation—locks her new child in the big, tall, stairless tower she just happens to have in the backyard.

Rapunzel spends her days up in the tower doing, well, whatever you do when you're locked in a tower 24/7. (Answer: The Jumble.) Each day is highlighted when the crazy gal shows up outside the window and demands admission by speaking the most famous entry request phrase in fairy tale history. ("Little pig, little pig—let me come in.") Rapunzel, of course, responds by letting down her exceptionally long hair (which one hopes does not refer to the hair on her "chinny-chin-chin") so the wacky lady can climb up for a visit.

One day, a prince comes riding by on horseback. He hears Rapunzel at the window having a little one-person tower sing-along, probably rapping some Eminem or something like that. He is immediately enchanted by her voice, but, lacking access to high-quality pole vaulting equipment, has no way to get up to Rapunzel's window. Instead, he is forced to hide in the bushes with his binoculars until he can figure out how the woman makes her daily entrance.

Once Prince Peeping Tom finally learns the magic words to gain admission, he tricks Rapunzel into dropping her tresses for him instead. They immediately hit it off (actually, in one version of the story he knocks her up, so maybe her hair wasn't the only thing she was dropping) and begin plotting how to bust Rapunzel out so they can live happily ever after. Unfortunately, neither of these two is exactly a physics wizard, so this is a bit of a struggle. They devise some sort of plan where the prince will smuggle silk up to Rapunzel until she has enough to make a ladder and climb down to freedom. Okay, Einsteins.

Of course, this plan doesn't come even close to working. The crazy lady catches on to the scheme and responds by chopping off Rapunzel's hair and booting her out on her ass to live in the woods. The lady then lures the prince up the leftover locks, gives him the bad news that his girlfriend is gone, and throws him back out the window and into a big pile of thorns where he ends up blind. Kind of a shitty day for him.

But not all is lost. After some time being one with nature and bumping into a lot of trees, one day he hears a familiar voice busting rhymes and belting out Kanye West lyrics. The lovers are soon reunited. Then, in a very convenient bonus, Rapunzel starts crying, and damned if her tears don't cure blindness. Suddenly the prince can see again, and he and Rapunzel ride off into the sunset—either to rule his kingdom, or maybe to open up a roadside stand selling radishes.

Rumpelstiltskin

A local miller gets into a chat with the king (because those two people obviously are bumping into each other at Home Depot every day), and idly slips into the conversation that, "Oh, you know, my daughter just happens to be able to spin straw into gold."

Well, that's a useful talent. Explains why your family is doing so well and you are working as a miller.

Regardless, the brainiac king is intrigued. He sends for the girl, locks her in a tower (tower-locking is becoming a theme here), and tells her that she has three days to spin up some bling or he's going to kill her. So that all worked out pretty well. Thanks, Dad.

In a stunning plot twist, we soon learn that the daughter actually *cannot* make gold out of straw. She is, however, quite good at crying, and bawls for a good two days—right until a tiny little man suddenly appears in the tower with her. Quite conveniently, this particular little fellow has a special talent: spinning straw into gold. He agrees to spin for her—multiple times—but it's not like he works for free. Instead, each time he trades off his efforts for an ever-escalating list of personal items: necklaces, rings, Justin Bieber tickets, etc.

As the little guy churns out loot, the girl sends it along to the king and passes it off as her own. But instead of praising her fine work, His Highness just keeps expanding his demands. One day the girl runs out of things to barter with Sir Spinalot, leading the gnome-dude to say he'll spin one more time—in exchange for her first-born child. Knowing that she actually had a kid five years earlier who turned out to be a total little shit, she immediately agrees.

The diminutive fella spins up a final load, and the miller's daughter delivers the finished gold. The king responds, as any logical person would, by immediately marrying her. Nine months later, she delivers a child. (Way to go, King!) No sooner has the rabbi finished up the kid's circumcision than the mysterious little man reappears to pick up his payment. The new Mrs. King is distraught. But then, in a deft negotiating maneuver they only teach in the most expensive seminars, Tiny says that he'll let her out of the whole deal if she can guess his name in three days. Wait, whaaaaat?

The man comes back each of the next two days, allowing the girl to guess as many times as she wants. She fires off every name she can think of herself, consults www.dumbbabynames.com, and even calls up Gwyneth Paltrow to see if she's had any bright ideas recently. (Gwyneth couldn't take the call because Apple was at ballet class.) No luck. With one day left, the baby is on the verge of immediately becoming the tallest member of his new household.

At this point in the story, many folks believe that the queen's neck gets saved when her messenger stumbles on to the little man chanting his name around a campfire. C'mon, people, let's be realistic here. In the real world, pint-sized elf men that can spin straw into gold don't go around name-checking themselves at campfires like they're making a hip hop record. Truth is, the small fry just goes out to the bar that night, and the royal bouncer is so convinced that his "Rumpelstiltskin" ID is a fake that he calls the palace in hopes this might be an offense worthy of the dungeon. That's the real story.

News of the possible name quickly gets back to the queen. She's skeptical, but it's not like she has any better ideas. When the little man shows up the next day and confirms he does not go by either "McLovin" or "Carlos Danger," the queen suggests "well, then maybe your name is Rumpelstiltskin."

Somehow the Royal Name Police confirm that queenie is correct, and her baby is forever saved from a life with a father that has an endless supply of gold. Cause that sure would suck. Shorty, on the other hand, is not pleased by this unexpected development. Depending upon the version of the story, he either a) stomps his foot into the ground so hard it gets stuck, b) physically tears himself in half, or c) runs off, never to be seen again (but later is rumored to have joined a carnival running the "I'll guess your name or you win a free stuffed animal" booth).

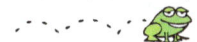

Jack and the Beanstalk

Demonstrating a level of business sense normally reserved for dim-witted gophers and members of the Cleveland Browns front office, a poor English farm boy named Jack goes to the market and trades his family's last cow for a handful of allegedly "magic" beans. When he comes home and tells his mom about his shrewd wheeling and dealing, let's just say mama is less than thrilled. After taking a moment to write Jack out of the will, she chucks the beans out the window in frustration.

Shockingly, however, the magical legumes turn out to work as advertised. Jack and his mom wake up the next morning to find that a giant beanstalk has sprouted in their yard like a mutant dandelion.

Despite his mother's suggestion to just spray the damn thing with Roundup, Jack knows better. Thanks to his extensive background playing Super Mario Brothers as a kid, he understands that when you see a beanstalk going up into the clouds, the correct action is to immediately climb it. Up he goes, but instead of being able to warp to World 8, Jack runs headlong into a pissy, hungry giant who is soon Fee-Fi-Fo-Fumming upon discovering his unexpected visitor.

Now many people, faced with a situation like this, would probably turn around and walk away. To be fair, however, others might run like hell. But not our Jack. He opts for choice three—rob the giant that is trying to eat you.

With some covert assistance from Jumbo's wife, Jack makes off with a couple of sacks of gold, a hen that lays golden eggs, and the giant's prized collection of dryer lint. Rather than stop there, Jack makes one final trip up the beanstalk, completing the heist by hauling off with a magic harp that plays its own songs. Because those are obviously in high demand. Turns out, however, that this particular harp also speaks (why not?), and it soon calls out to the giant asking to be rescued.

Dragging the loudmouth harp along, Jack frantically clambers down the beanstalk with the giant in hot pursuit. Upon reaching the bottom, Jack busts out an ax and chops the stalk to the ground. The giant tumbles to his death, leaving behind a big-ass hole (not to be confused with a big asshole).

Danger now averted, Jack returns to everyday life taking care of his mother. He also snags himself a sugar-mama by marrying the giant's cougar wife, and they make millions selling As Seen On TV™ golden-egg-laying hens and singing harps. They keep the dryer lint—after all, you never know when the Guinness Book of Records might come calling.

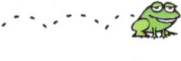

Hungry Captain Hook Wonders if Peter Pan Will be Creamy or Crunchy

Caesar Commissions "Emperor's New Jock Strap"

Pleased with the public response to his "new clothes," Emperor Randy Caesar has requested that his tailors immediately go to work to design a custom athletic supporter for his upcoming role as the starting catcher on the imperial fast-pitch softball team. Caesar issued a press release yesterday, declaring "after their fine craftsmanship on my wardrobe, these are the guys I want protecting my 'guys.'"

The Emperor's statement also addressed complaints from some of the country's "simpler" citizens that couldn't see the new clothes during his parade last week. After consulting former advisors to Bill Clinton, Caesar apologized for seeming to appear naked, but maintained it was really no big deal because, "I didn't gyrate."

More Difficulties for Trump's London Bridge Repair Project

The signature piece of President Donald Trump's infrastructure plan, the quest to repair Arizona's crumbling London Bridge, continues to frustrate architects, as another round of structural enhancements has gone sour. Trump made repairing the dilapidated span a priority after his election, but the effort has been a struggle. After multiple failures, the White House most recently attempted to build the falling bridge up with "some tremendous pins and needles." Engineers, however, later discovered that pins and needles rust and bend, and apparently are not well suited for buttressing a bridge.

The team's first effort, involving iron bars, fell apart when the bars bent and broke immediately after crews attached the "M" of the giant "T-R-U-M-P" that the Mr. Trump had requested be placed on the bridge's north side. Trump tweeted yesterday that he has sent his designers back to devise another plan, which sources indicate may involve reinforcing the bridgework with Trump's hair.

...TV Today

3 PM - Montel Williams - Less Famous Siblings
Montel continues his series reuniting celebrities with their siblings that didn't make the big time. Peter Peter Pumpkineater's brother, Rod Rod the Rhubarb God, is profiled.

4 PM - Maury Povich - Who's The Daddy? - The Ugly Duckling
The Ugly Duckling learns the results of another of Maury's trademark paternity tests, finding out once and for all how the hell he was born a baby duck yet somehow grew up into a swan.

5 PM - Judge Judy - Jenkins vs. Old Woman
A landlord sues his tenant for failure to pay rent on the shoe she and her many children are leasing.

Snow White

A beautiful young princess draws the ire of her stepmother when the queen's talking mirror identifies this "Snow White" as the "fairest of them all"—whatever the hell that means. To deal with this inconvenience, the queen hires a hunter, possibly Dick Cheney, to take Snow White into the woods and dispose of her.

Now this all sounds like a great idea, but when push comes to shove, the hunter doesn't have the stones to finish the job (so maybe it wasn't Cheney after all). He instead figures he can still collect his paycheck, and avoid execution, so long as he brings a deer heart back to the queen to convince her the deed was done. He tells Snow White to hide in the forest and then, in a brilliant Disney cross-promotion, shoots Bambi's mom and takes her heart back to dupe the queen.

Following the hunter's instructions, Snow White aimlessly wanders around the woods for a while. She eventually shacks up with seven slob miners with names like "Sleepy," "Sweaty," and "Dufus," all of whom would still be shorter than Tom Cruise if you stacked them on top of each other. Snow White soon takes over the cooking and cleaning duties in the dwarf frat house. This doesn't exactly do wonders for women's gender roles in society, but it does greatly improve the living conditions, which previously were about on par with what you would expect at your local Motel 6. The dwarfs, on the other hand, spend most of their time walking back and forth to work while singing "Hi, Ho!" to greet the various prostitutes they pass along the way.

This whole arrangement works out splendidly, at least until the queen's mirror spills the beans that Snow White is still alive. The queen is none too pleased. She dons her scariest Bea Arthur costume, tracks down Snow White, and gives her a complimentary poisoned candy apple. Snow White bites into the apple with the gusto of an old lady in a denture adhesive commercial, immediately knocking herself into a catatonic state of suspended animation. On the plus side, however, her dwarf roomies are so kind as to put her on display in a glass coffin outside their house. Because that's not weird. (They also take the time to send the evil queen tumbling off a cliff to her death. No glass coffin for her, though.)

Now you might think that having a group of little people keeping a semi-dead woman a glass box in their yard would make this story awkward enough. But you'd be wrong, as things next go straight to a level of weirdness normally reserved only for the U.S. Senate Halloween Party. Noted good Samaritan Prince Charming comes riding by, spots the comatose lady, and promptly decides that the best way to assist would be to dismount and give this gal a kiss.

While I doubt that this form of roadside assistance is the kind of "jump start" AAA recommends, you have to admit, it's pretty effective. Snow White suddenly jolts wide awake, good as new. Next thing you know, the two of them fall in love, ride off into the sunset, and live happily ever after. Blah, blah, blah…

Sleeping

A king and queen welcome a new bundle of joy into their lives, and, lacking any actual good ideas for a name, call their baby girl Aurora. As any responsible parents would, they summon a group of fairies to come bless their new daughter. Due to some typos on the guest list, however, an evil fairy gets past security and curses the baby to die if she pricks her finger on a spinning wheel on her 16th birthday. Not exactly what the king and queen had in mind.

After a quick panic, one of the backup fairies on site steps in and waters down the curse so that Aurora will not actually die from the pricking, but instead will just fall asleep—maybe for 100 years, maybe until she's kissed by a true love, or perhaps until the extended warranty on the castle daybed expires. Regardless, it's safe to say she won't need to refill her Ambien prescription any time soon.

Now, this is just me, but if I knew that my daughter would be cursed if she got pricked on a spinning wheel on her 16th birthday, I might be inclined to mention that piece of information and advise her to "stay the hell away from spinning wheels on your birthday." Of course, nobody has been knocking on my door asking me to become king lately, so what do I know? The real king instead takes the genius step of banning spinning wheels throughout the kingdom, which of course means that everybody and their uncle has to immediately go out and get one off Craig's List to hide in their basement. Great work, King. Go buy yourself a "Number One Dad" t-shirt.

Time passes and Aurora grows up. After a bustling childhood that may have involved mov-

Beauty

ing in with the good fairies and possibly adopting the stage name Briar Rose, she reaches her 16th birthday. And damn if she doesn't just happen to stumble onto a woman using a curious looking wheel to make yarn. "Wanna try?" "Sure." "Go ahead." "Ow—zzzzzzzzzzzzzzzzzzzzzzzzzzzz."

Aurora, a.k.a. Sleeping Beauty, is zonked out like your dad after Thanksgiving dinner. At this point, one of the good fairies finally shows up (clearly having done a fine job of preventing disaster thus far) and decides the best way to deal with the situation would be to put everyone else in the kingdom to sleep, too. So now we've got the entire country comatose. Hope none of the neighbors have an invasion on the calendar any time soon. Also, if you're watching the movie, this would be an excellent time to run to the fridge. You won't miss much.

Years in the future, Sleeping Beauty gets a wake up call in the form of a kiss from a neighboring prince, who either just randomly showed up, or maybe first went through the trouble of killing off the bad fairy while she was disguised as a dragon. Check your local listings. (On a side note, between Snow White and Sleeping Beauty, it seems to me like hospitals could save a lot of time and expense by hiring a kissing prince for every emergency room. Who needs an AED to save lives if you can just station some royalty in the waiting area?)

Anyway, Aurora wakes up, as does everyone else. That's pretty much it. She and her new prince live happily ever after, bringing their kingdom great new riches thanks mainly to her new endorsement deal with 5-Hour Energy. Life is good.

Emperor Drops Off His Old Clothes at Goodwill

The Little Red Hen

In this story, it looks like we have the Little Red Hen wanting to make some bread, only to be shocked when none of the other creatures and critters in town will help her with the project. Now let's think about this for a second. What kind of lazy-ass bum needs helpers for this job? We're making bread here, people. No need for a factory assembly line. I mean, what exactly was she asking? "Who will help me flip the on/off switch on my oven?"

Seems to me that the Little Red Hen was pretty much nagging the hell out of everyone in town. Probably a bit tired from her most recent request for assistance tying her shoelaces, the other animals were just dishing out some much-needed tough love by refusing to assist.

Eventually Ms. Hen storms home in a huff, resigned that she will have to do the work herself. After a couple of surely exhausting hours of staring at her breadmaker, she returns, asking everyone, "Who will help me eat my bread?" This time they accept her offer—but surely just out of sympathy. After all, it's a little tough to believe that the Little Red Hen was cooking up anything that would rival the local bakery (or the local gas station, for that matter).

Despite their courtesy, she sticks her beak in the air and tells them, "Hell no, bitches. You don't help, you don't eat." As the other animals secretly breathe a collective sigh of relief, the hen struts home to enjoy the spoils of her "hard" work. She's still stuck on her porch to this day, however, since so far nobody has agreed to come open her door for her.

The Ugly Duckling

This is not the most complicated story you've ever heard. There's this baby duck. He's ugly. So nobody likes him. Especially not his brothers and sisters. Then he grows up into a beautiful swan. This means he can fly over his brothers and sisters and take enormous shits on them. I'm sure there's an important moral lesson here somewhere.

Family Members Panic-Stricken After Humpty Dumpty Wins Trip to Great Wall of China on Game Show

The Princess

A prince is on the prowl for a bride, but seems to be having a problem finding himself a real princess. Must have been a major fraudulent royalty epidemic going on around these parts at the time. (This could also be a "flatulent royalty epidemic" if you happen to be a poor typist.)

One particular night, a monstrous rainstorm hits. Soon there's a knock at the castle door, and the king and queen answer it to find a bedraggled woman soaking wet on their doorstep. She is desperate to get in out of the storm and asks if she can stay the night. Since she left her AAA card at home and the castle doesn't seem to offer an AARP discount, she tries the old "Oh, by the way, I'm a princess" routine in hopes of securing nicer accommodations.

This claim gets the queen's attention, as apparently she was thinking that the drowned rat on her porch would make a nice catch for the prince—but only if she's a real princess. Utilizing the secret international protocol for princess testing, the queen invites the girl to stay, then proceeds to stack up 20 or so mattresses on top of a single pea in the girl's bedroom. (She also sets the Sleep Number on the top mattress to 97.)

The girl heads to bed, somehow not finding it odd that she has to scale an extension ladder balanced on top of a trampoline just to hit the sack. She actually sleeps like a log, but, hoping to add a complimentary breakfast to her free stay, claims that she tossed and turned all night and ended up just watching reruns of *Mr. Belvedere* on the room tv. The queen logically assumes that the lady couldn't sleep because she is so incredibly sensitive that she felt the pea, and further concludes that the only person who could be so delicate is a real princess. (Seems safe to bet that Sleeping Beauty won't be marrying into this family any time soon.)

Based upon this brilliant deduction, the queen is completely convinced that this drenched and possibly homeless traveler is the perfect person to marry her son. The girl, of course, thinks this plan is just fine—this is no time for her to hop off the gravy train—and the prince is shockingly on board as well. So they get hitched, just like that. And hopefully get separate beds at the palace.

and the Pea

The Three Billy Goats Gruff

Three billy goat brothers, all named "Gruff," find that their meadow has been paved over to build a new Starbucks, and take off one-by-one on a hike to greener pastures. The trip requires crossing a rickety old hanging bridge, the kind you usually only see in Indiana Jones-style movies when the hero is being chased by some sort of demon-possessed tomato plant.

The smallest goat arrives at the bridge first and decides to take a shot at crossing. Just as he begins to trip-trap-trip-trap across, he runs into a very ugly, very angry, very hungry troll (or, in some alternate translations, Jack Nicholson). The troll announces that he is ready for lunch, but Gruff suggests that the troll should wait for his bigger, fatter, tastier brother, who will be coming along shortly. The troll, being a troll and all, falls for this. (Either that, or he thought this was one of those delayed-gratification psychology experiments where if you hold out until the end they give you a free pizza.)

Right on cue, a few minutes later, a fatter goat trip-traps up to the bridge. Seeing that his skinny brother has crossed without difficulty, Gruff Jr. starts heading to the other side as well. The troll appears and declares the goat-buffet open for business, but again finds his lunch put on hold when he is tempted by the promise of an even meatier goat coming along soon. The second goat also passes without incident.

Finally, to the troll's delight, Gruff 3.0 arrives. As promised, this goat is huge. However, lost in the fine print of the previous brother's offer is the fact that this goat uses the same steroid dealer as Barry Bonds, and therefore is jacked. Plus, he's got horns. The next thing you know the troll is flying off the bridge, and the mega-goat trip-traps off to join his brothers and munch grass happily ever after. At least until Indiana Jones and the demonic tomatoes get there.

Simple Simon Clarifies, Says He's Actually a Thigh Man

THE BREMEN TOWN MUSICIANS

Who the f--- cares?

Amish Fairy Godmother Turns Ferrari
Into Horse-Drawn Carriage

The Three Little Pigs

Stunned after their mother is killed in a tragic back-alley run-in with Oscar Mayer, three orphan pig brothers are abruptly thrust out into the world on their own. In need of lodging, they each decide to build their own house. Because that's always a fun and rewarding experience. At least they know enough not to hire a contractor.

Pig 1 steps up to bat first, and, showing all of the drive and initiative of a disgruntled DMV employee, decides to build his house out of straw. Not straws. Straw. Probably not up to code.

Undaunted by the rustic accommodations, he moves into his new digs. However, having failed to sign up for the neighborhood watch, Pig 1 soon finds the Big Bad Wolf on his porch asking to come in for a visit. Proving to at least be better at judging character than selecting building materials (or maybe just suspicious that the wolf could be a Jehovah's Witness wanting to chat), the pig promptly says "no way." The wolf responds by huffing, puffing, and blowing the house down—not exactly a major task in light of the construction. Pig 1 runs for his life.

Pig 2 hears about his brother's plight, and quickly realizes that building your house out of straw is pretty damn stupid. Obviously any hog worth his weight in bacon bits would use something more durable. Such as sticks. So Pig 2 builds himself a lovely stick cabin.

Alas, when it comes to building a cabin by hand, this pig is no Abraham Lincoln (insert Abra"HAM" pig joke here). The house of sticks is not exactly what you would call an architectural triumph. The Big Bad Wolf shows up for the housewarming party, gets shut outside, and promptly blows the place to the ground. Pig 2 heads for the hills. (As a side note, he is still battling with his homeowner's insurance as to whether this incident qualifies as "wind damage.")

Pig 1 and Pig 2 make their way over to Pig 3's place, which he has built out of bricks. Pig 3 is what we call an overachiever. When the wolf shows up and delivers a Category Five hurricane force blow, the house doesn't budge. Undeterred, the wolf gets the stepladder out of his truck and heads for the roof. But by the time he starts sliding down the chimney, the pigs have stoked the flames and put their Rachael Ray Signature Edition Giant Wolf Cooking Pot into the fireplace. The wolf crash-lands into his new personal hot tub and quickly gets served up for dinner.[1] As for the pigs, one assumes that two out of three are now living happily ever after. And that Pig 3 is about ready to blow someone's oinker off wondering if his stupid brothers are ever going to move out.

---

[1] Actually, while most folks assume that the pigs ate the wolf, rumors persist that he actually survived and went on to eat Little Red Riding Hood and her grandmother. According to the *National Enquirer*, he recently was seen at a Burger King in Kalamazoo, Michigan, riding in a blue van being driven by Elvis. He's also rumored to be working on a new autobiography with O.J. Simpson's ghostwriter titled *If I Ate Them, Here's How They Tasted*.

BAD TIMING

The Fox and the Hound

Tod and Copper. A bromance between a fox and a dog. Sure, why not?

Our story begins when Tod the fox gets adopted by a crazy old lady whose vision is so bad that she can't tell the difference between a fox and a puppy. (She also doesn't know how to spell Todd.) She lives next door to a mountain man named Amos Slade, which makes him sound like he should either be a rock star or a Supreme Court Justice. Justice Slade has an old-fart tracking dog named Chief, whose nose has deteriorated to the point that pretty much the only smell he can track *is* farts. (It wasn't me. Honest.) Slade decides it's time for a canine upgrade, and picks out a new hound dog puppy named Copper.

Shortly after Copper's arrival, Tod wanders next door to say hello. The two of them hit it off, and only later does Copper find out that his job, his *only* job, is to hunt for Tod. Oops. Next time, read the contract more carefully.

A few days later, Slade notices Tod swinging by for a play date, and sets his tracking team off to catch him some fox. To his own dismay, Copper corners Tod almost immediately. He tries to let his buddy go, but Chief inconveniently chooses this moment to be the first time in years for his nose to actually work and picks up Tod's trail himself.

Of course, smelling is one thing, chasing is another. While Chief is in hot pursuit, he wipes out, breaks his leg, and maybe dies. Depends on whose version you're reading. (Well, that and the fact that at Chief's geezer-dog energy levels, "dead" and "not dead" look basically the same.)

In just a small overreaction, Copper then blames Tod for everything bad that ever happened to Chief. Copper and Slade set off to kick Tod's ass, forcing the old lady to move Tod into a protected game preserve. That works—for about five minutes. Then Tod again finds himself on the run from a Slade and Copper poaching expedition. Security at this game preserve . . . not too impressive.

Equally unimpressive, however, are Slade and Copper's stealth hunting skills. First, their sneak attack attracts the attention of a nearby bear. Then, as the grizzly starts mauling Copper, Slade the Hunting Wizard catches himself in one of his Tod Traps. (Copper seriously might want to get on LinkedIn and start looking for a more talented employer.) While Slade is trying to find the release button, Tod the Adolescent Fox emerges from the weeds and saves the day by opening up a can of Whoop-Ass on the fully grown bear in one of your more plausible fight matchups.

Tod is rewarded for his heroism when an injured Slade comes up and tries to shoot him anyway. Copper, however, is not going to have it. He stands over Tod's injured body to take the bullet, Secret Service style. Slade, of course, just blows Copper away, figuring he can buy himself a new dog once the damn fox is out of the picture. Okay, not really. Slade doesn't shoot, and Copper drags the old man home so the wacky old lady next door can nurse him back to health. Knowing that his friendship with Copper can't continue (except maybe as an NBC sitcom), Tod stays behind in the game preserve and shacks up with a new lady friend. They probably have a kid named Chadd just to even up the d's.

Paul Bunyan Suffering From Really Huge Bunions

Hare Named Winner After Tortoise Fails Post-Race Drug Test

United Airlines Clarifies: She'll Be Comin' Round the Mountain About 45 Minutes Late

Court News:
Young Boy Changes Name

A local 12-year-old boy is learning a new signature today after successfully petitioning the Superior Court to change his name. Formerly known as Jack Sprat, Jr., the boy snuck away from his famously skinny father just long enough to file the request to change his name to Jack Sproccoli. Asked by Judge Stewart McDougal why he wanted to do so, the boy pointed out that now "Jack Sproccoli" will "eat no broccoli."

In a separate petition, "Rumpelstiltskin Jones" changed his name to "Dave Jones."

Third Little Piggy's Requests for Roast Beef Causing Tension with Steers in Barnyard

Little Red Hen Outsources Bread Making Operation to China

Farmer in the Dell Returns Wife He Took

Mary Obtains Restraining Order Against Stalker Lamb

THE GINGERBREAD MAN

The Gingerbread Man, everyone's favorite trash-talking dessert, escapes from the senior citizens that made him by taking off on the run the moment they open the oven door. He heads out of the house, taunting the old folks on his way out by saying "Run, run, as fast as you can! You can't catch me, you're a slow ass old man! And you're riding one of those Rascal scooters!"

As he heads down the road, Mr. Gingerbread soon runs into a chatty, not to mention hungry, cow. Bessie points out that the Gingerbread Man looks quite delicious, but he sprints away before she can turn him into lunch. He has a similar meeting with a less-than-speedy horse, as well as a fleet-footed . . . chicken. Makes you wonder what kind of funny brownies the original authors had been baking in their own ovens when they worked out this list of animals.

Soon the Gingerbread Man is cruising along with half of Old McDonald's Farm giving chase. A dilemma arises, however, when his road dead-ends at a river. Since the old man and woman forgot to bake a set of floaties onto his arms, this poses a serious problem. But not to worry. A fox is waiting at the river's edge, and he points out that he just happens to be offering free water taxi service (and that he has no interest in any ginger-based desserts whatsoever).

With a buffoonish naïveté you would normally expect only from the Pillsbury Doughboy, the Gingerbread Man confidently hops on the fox's back. He similarly does not bat an eye when the fox claims that the water is getting deep, so it would be wise to jump right up on the tip of his nose. And then, with a quick toss and a snap of the jaws . . . no more Gingerbread Man.

(Unfortunately for the fox, the Gingerbread Man turns out to be undercooked, and Captain Foxy comes down with a violent case of food poisoning. Add to that the fact that he didn't wait an hour after eating before going for a swim, and the fox ends up projectile vomiting gingerbread body parts all over the place. That detail seems to get left out of the story books.)

The Tortoise and the Hare

David killing Goliath. The 1980 U.S. Olympic Hockey Team beating Russia. That one time my dad and I won a game of *Pictionary*. History is full of stunning victories that simply cannot be explained by common sense. But none of them rival the biggest upset of all time—the Tortoise over the Hare.

Now I'm not sure how anyone even thought to set up a race with the approximate competitive balance of Usain Bolt vs. Walter Cronkite. Nonetheless, the battle is soon on, and the Hare bursts out of the starting gate like Secretariat. The Tortoise, on the other hand, gets started more like the secretary at CementWorld—if there had been an incident involving some of the merchandise. "Slow and steady wins the race," the Tortoise declares, ranking right up there with "I did not have sexual relations with that woman" on the list of the world's most ridiculous claims.

In what seems like the blink of an eye, the Hare is closing in on the finish line. Of course, it's not enough for him to just win going away, so he decides to deliver a solid "up yours" to the Tortoise by lying down and taking a nap in the road a few feet short of the checkered flag.

The term "nap," however, turns out to be a bit of an understatement. Either the Hare was related to Rip Van Winkle or he'd just pulled an all-nighter, because in about ten seconds, he's OUT. Gone. Good night.

While the Hare snoozes the day away, the Tortoise plods down the course at top speed, pausing only to watch giant sequoias sprout up around him, various species fade into extinction, and Halley's Comet visit the Earth a couple of times. Eventually, though, he cruises past the still snoring Hare and crosses the finish line as the winner, delighting the crowd members' great-grandchildren. He is thrilled by his victory and offers many more inspiring nuggets of wisdom to the youth of America, or at least we assume he will if he ever makes it over to the media center for his post-race press conference.

Your Local AFLAC Agent
Humpty Dumpty
→ Former customer
→ 15 years experience
→ Ask me about my top-rated Accident Policy

supplemental insurance

AFLAC covers you for:
→ Slips
→ Falls
→ Broken Bones
→ Incontinence
→ Impotence
→ Dwarfism
→ Elephantiasis
→ Dandruff
→ Herpes
→ Paper Cuts
→ Turning into a Frog

It's not just for 7-fingered shop teachers anymore!

ABC's Bachelor Makes His Choice

The 47th installment of ABC's reality dating show *The Bachelor* came to an end last night, as Bachelor Georgie Porgie proposed to florist Mary M. Quite-Contrary. Porgie was one of the most entertaining Bachelors in the show's history, kissing 23 of the 25 women over the course of the season and leaving many of them in tears. In the final episode, Porgie shocked Contrary by reaching into his pants and whipping out an 8-inch cockle shell, which he presented to Mary along with a ring.

Despite the show's abysmal track record, host Chris Harrison expressed confidence in the new couple's prospects. "This time it's true love for sure," he told a TMZ reporter, while simultaneously purchasing a copy of US Weekly that claimed that Porgie was actually having a secret affair with Contrary's aunt's hairdresser's horse. Executive producer Mike Fleiss echoed Harrison's sentiment with a nearly straight face before adding, "Oh, come on. Who the hell are we trying to kid here?"

MARY HAD A LITTLE SPAM...

Little Red Riding Hood

Little Red Riding Hood, a young lady who clearly could use a bit of fashion advice, sets off to take some food to her ailing grandmother. It appears that Medicaid would only spring for a nursing home located in the middle of a deserted forest, however, so the trip is quite the excursion for our young lady.

As Little Red dusts off her cape and departs, her mother (Big Red) warns her to follow her phone's GPS and stay on the beaten path. Well, we all know how well advice like that usually works out. Little Red makes it about four steps down the road before she starts traipsing all over the place. She soon meets up with a talking wolf, which must be an everyday occurrence in these parts, since she doesn't seem too phased by the development. The wolf, meanwhile, figures that this girl would make a nice lunch, and strikes up a conversation with his newfound tasty morsel. During their discussion, Little Red prudently mentions that she's traveling solo, then goes on to disclose her precise destination, credit card information, social security number, and Facebook password. She apologizes when she can't remember how to spell her mother's maiden name.

Before they go their separate ways, the wolf convinces Little Red that any good granddaughter would surely stop and pick some flowers before going on to Grandma's. This gives him plenty of time to race ahead, gobble down Gran with a side of fries, put on her clothes, and get into her bed. (This does make you wonder—did the wolf somehow convince Grandma to take all of her clothes off before he ate her? Seems like an awkward request to make. Just thinking out loud here.)

Little Red arrives a few minutes later, flowers in hand, and promptly demonstrates that her extraordinary stupidity is rivaled only by her prodigiously poor vision. Red starts to catch up on old times with "Grandma," not picking up on the minor detail that her grandmother has been replaced by a wolf—at least not until he starts using his "better to eat you with" teeth to snarf her down for dessert.

At just this moment (rather good timing), a hunter saunters by and decides it would be wise to trespass inside the grandmother's place just to see if anything might be amiss. Not only that, but this particular hunter also happens to be an amateur veterinary surgeon, and he immediately performs a MacGyver-style operation with Granny's knitting needles to extract Little Red and her grandmother from the wolf's stomach unharmed. Piece of cake. Now, who's ready for dinner?

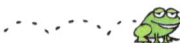

Old McDonald Struggles on Wheel of Fortune After Only Buying Vowels

Robin Hood

If you like people with a girl's name, a varied supply of hosiery, and a reputation for robbing the rich to give to the poor, then Nancy Pelosi is probably the congresswoman for you.

No. Hold on. I read my notes wrong. Actually, if you like those things, then Robin Hood might be the medieval bandit for you. That's it. He hangs out in the beautiful Sherwood Forest with his group of "Merry Men," including Little John, Friar Tuck, and Richard Simmons, plus their housekeeper, Marian the Maid. The whole robbing the rich to give to the poor deal turns out to be a pretty useful company policy for them—mainly considering the fact that they were ALL POOR.

They spend their days stealing from the dastardly Prince John and outrunning the witless Sheriff of Nottingham, who may have been some sort of distant ancestor of Barney Fife. This goes on for a while until Prince John's brother, King Richard, finally returns from his long trip overseas to star in a Shakespearean play. King Dick puts Prince John back in his place, elevates Robin to hero status, and sells the movie rights to Disney on the condition that he will be played by a lion—preferably Mufasa. All is well.

Web Opinion Poll

Yesterday's Question:
Who do you think was the "Someone" in the kitchen with Dinah?

Your votes:
Bill Clinton	49%
Charlie Sheen	31%
Tiger Woods	16%
Larry King	4%

Today's Question:
Does "strumming on the old banjo" count as sex?

Typo-ridden Publisher Accidentally Releases "The Aunt and the Asshopper"

Muffin Man, Muffler Man to Exchange Lives in Hilarious New Reality Show

Costco Staff Nervous as Rapunzel Heads Toward Shampoo Aisle

Stories You Don't Remember

Let's be honest here. I hope you remember the basics of what happened in most of these stories. If you've purchased or shoplifted this book to find out what the whole deal with Goldilocks and those bears was all about, there are probably better uses for your time. Including semi-pro badminton.

That being said, some of the details of your lesser-known fairy tales and legends may be elusive to the average person on the street, and I figure it's my responsibility to fill in the gaps. To determine which stories might need this kind of coverage, I have conducted cutting-edge scientific research by looking at a list of fairy tales and putting check marks next to the ones where I had to look up the details online to remember what happened. Such as . . .

Lady Godiva

Long before the Tea Party cornered the market on complaining about high taxes (and occasionally nominating someone who might be a witch to run for Congress), there was only one name in anti-tax demonstrations: Lady Godiva.

Prior to getting into the business of making really expensive chocolates, Mrs. Godiva was the world's first and hottest tax protester. According to the story, her husband, Barack Godiva, was taxing the balls out of the good folks of Coventry, and Lady Godiva didn't like it. Thus, in an act sure to lower taxes (or at least raise public morale), Lady G. took off riding a horse through town—buck naked. Mr. Godiva turned into Ronald Reagan by the next morning.

Today, it seems that this particular method of tax protest has fallen out of favor. That's disappointing, because I bet there's a lot of Hooter's waitresses who hate high taxes. On the other hand, maybe it's for the best. Nobody really wants to see Mitch McConnell galloping through the streets of D.C. in the buff. (Somebody remind him to watch out for the saddle horn.)

Rip Van Winkle

Rip Van Winkle falls asleep for a damn long time. You probably remember that part. But do you remember why? Me neither.

Apparently, one day in the 1770s, Rip tells his old lady that he is headed out for a while. He goes off for a walk in the mountains, and along the way bumps into a man carrying a giant keg. Starting to look like a good day for the Ripster. He follows this man up the mountain, where they come upon a whole group of dudes doing some good old-fashioned outdoor hilltop bowling. Who are these mystery men, you ask? The ghosts of the crew of the famous explorer Henry Hudson, of course. Duh. And what do these ghost men do next? They get old Rip wasted on their booze. As in, "pass-out-for-20-years" wasted.

So yes, you've got this straight. The guy sneaks out to get away from his nagging wife, doesn't come home for twenty years, and the best story he can think up in that time is that he got roofied by a team of boozer bowling explorer ghosts. Obviously.

The Town Mouse and the Country Mouse

This is the story where the high-falutin town mouse goes to visit his country cousin and declares everything out in the country to be dull as hell. He then invites the country mouse to come see him in the big city so he can show off. The country mouse shows up, and they promptly get chased by a big dog. The country mouse decides that the city sucks. This is the most boring fairy tale ever.

Tom Thumbelina

If you're a shorty that wants to feel like a giant, Tom Thumb and Thumbelina are the stories for you. Here's all you really need to know to tell them apart. Thumbelina is the one who lived on a lily pad and had to turn down opportunities to marry a toad and a mole. Tom Thumb got eaten by a cow, only to be saved when people gave the cow a laxative (Cowrectol, perhaps?) and got her to crap Tom out in a "cowturd." Honest. It's on the Internet. Even the actual word "cowturd." Google it.

The Little Mermaid

You likely know the main points here, once again thanks to your friend Wally Disney. We've basically got a mermaid who wants to become a human because she's got the hots for Mr. Prince up on the land. Regrettably, she fails the human citizenship test when she is unable to name at least three members of the cast of *Baywatch*. (The lack of legs might have been a problem, too.) Instead, she looks in the yellow pages and finds a sea witch, who offers to turn her into a human for the low, low price of: her voice. The witch also adds the condition that the mermaid will need to get the prince to fall in love with her if she wants to complete the transformation into a real human.

Armed with a set of feet, but no vocal cords, the mermaid heads ashore to tackle the task of silently wooing His Studliness. Somehow this almost works—at least until the prince gets tired of playing charades on every date. Eventually, though, the prince falls for another woman, who may or may not be the sea witch using the mermaid's stolen singing voice. Things are not going so well.

Now here's where you'll need to check your notes. If you prefer the Disney version, a singing crab, a fish, and a moron seagull come to the rescue just in time to prevent the prince from marrying the sea witch. The mermaid gets her voice back, marries the prince herself, and they live happily ever after. But, uh, well . . . bullshit. If you check out Hans Christian Andersen's original, the prince goes through with the original wedding and the mermaid just dies and dissolves into sea foam. Wow—great f---ing story, Hans. Maybe she came back as a can of that Scrubbing Bubbles cleanser or something.

The Ant and the Grasshopper

Here we have the story of an ant who spends his whole summer working, collecting food, lifting 300 times his own weight, etc. Meanwhile, his buddy, the do-nothing grasshopper, spends the summer singing. (Singing? Really? That's what they have the lazy insect do? Who writes this shit?) Winter comes, and, in a big stunner, MC Hopper suddenly finds himself getting very hungry.

The grasshopper goes to the ant and says, "Hey, buddy, how about some food for your hungry friend? I'll sing you a song." This is where things get good. Rather than caving in or being generous like your average annoying fairy tale character, the ant basically says "Screw off, Grasshopper" and slams the door, leaving the grasshopper to starve. End of story. (This is the favorite fairy tale of four out of five exterminators.)

The Sword in the Stone

Shortly after the death of the old king, a giant Acme Company anvil mysteriously appears in downtown London. This particular anvil has a sword sticking out of it, along with an inscription stating that whoever pulls the sword out of the stone gets to be the King of England. And will have a cool new sword.

One by one, men from around the world line up for some good old-fashioned sword yanking (not like that—get your head out of the gutter). Nobody can make it budge. In time, the sword is forgotten, and everyone goes about their lives getting the plague or whatever they did all day back then.

Meanwhile, we meet a young orphan kid with the unfortunate nickname of Wart. Wart spends most of his time training to be a squire, which as far as I can tell is basically a knight, just not as cool. (Think of it this way. Sir Paul McCartney = Knight. Ringo = Squire.)

One day, Wart heads off to assist his foster brother (Pustule) in a jousting tournament. As assistant, Wart has one job: bring the sword. So of course he forgets the sword. Gold star for you, buddy. He runs off to find a replacement, grabbing the first one he comes across (apparently there's a stray sword on every street corner in this neighborhood). Of course, the sword Wart finds just happens to be stuck in an anvil, but he pulls it out with ease. This delights the locals, who realize this is the famous sword in the stone, and that they finally have a king. Well, thank God for that. How did they ever survive without one?

Of course, he is not just any king. As everyone has long since figured out, this future owner of the sword Excalibur is no "Wart," but actually is none other than the famed Squire of the Round Table himself: Prince Charles.

Alice in Wonderland

I'm not feeling very motivated to write today. Let's see what Wikipedia has to say about this.

Alice in Wonderland   From Wikipedia, the free encyclopedia

> This article, like most of the crap here on Wikipedia, is full of unverified bulls--- that is barely more accurate than the meme your nutty cousin just posted on Facebook. But feel free to tell your friends about what you read here just like you saw it on *60 Minutes*. We really don't give a damn.

Alice Johnson (born October 8, 1954), better known as "Alice in Wonderland," is a ditsy literary character created by Lewis Carroll or Charles Dickens or one of those other famous British authors. You have never actually read the book, so don't even try to pretend you have, because nobody will believe you. Also, if you try to dress up like Alice for Halloween, you will probably end up looking like some sort of naughty milkmaid. But maybe you were going for that.

Visit to Wonderland

Bored out of her mind after spending the afternoon with her annoying sister, Alice travels to Wonderland (about 30 miles west of Topeka) in the normal way–following a talking rabbit down his hole, downing a beverage that shrinks you to a fraction of your normal size, and then slipping through a keyhole that doubles as Wonderland Customs. In the process, she also encounters some special cookies that instantly make you enormous ("Oreos"). More on those later.

Stop number one on the Wonderland tour is a "caucus race" directed by a dodo bird, where everyone runs around in a circle for hours (sorry, no passing) and nobody wins. This is an excellent activity for people who have not yet mastered the finer points of duck-duck-goose.

After taking a wrong turn down pit road, Alice decides she's had enough of the race and heads on her way. She soon meets up with a hookah-smoking caterpillar, and later encounters a Cheshire Cat. We have no idea what the hell a Cheshire Cat actually is, but we bet seeing it had something to do with Alice hitting the hookah.

The next stop on Alice's trip is a rendezvous with Tweedledee and Tweedledum, two boneheads who seem destined to be contestants on The Gong Show. They apparently enjoy poetry—at least if it involves walruses and/or carpenters.

At this point Alice needs a break, so she joins up with a nut job Mad Hatter, a different talking rabbit, and a wasted dormouse for a quick tea party. These three make that stoner caterpillar from earlier seem pretty damn normal. Alice also barfs after riding the spinning teacups.

Alice elects to wrap up her day with a quick game of croquet. Wonderland Croquet Supply must have recently gone out of business, since this particular game features flamingoes for mallets and a variety of hedgehogs in place of the balls. Basically we're talking about an advanced version of Whack-A-Mole. For an opponent, Alice draws the Queen of Hearts, who is pretty much a female Henry VIII, except with a shorter temper and more beheading equipment. Alice would be wise to not actually, you know, win.

Croquet completed, most people would head home and call it a day. Alice, however, gets waylaid when she gets herself put on trial for something or other. In a bold defense plan, she employs the time-honored legal strategy of eating Oreos until she's about a mile tall, then waking up and discovering that the whole thing was a bad dream. She later claims she learned this technique from an episode of the People's Court with Judge Wapner.

External Links

- Wonderland Tourism Bureau
- OK Croquet Monthly
- twitter.com – The_Real_Tweedledum – Official Twitter Page

Categories: People Who Talk To Caterpillars | Disappearing Cats | Milkmaids

Headless Horseman To Guest Star on *Sesame Street*

Sesame Street's lengthy list of celebrity guest stars increased by one yesterday, as producers announced that the legendary Headless Horseman will make a cameo on the show's upcoming season. The Horseman will warn youngsters about the dangers of decapitation, joining Cookie Monster for a rousing musical rendition of "G is for Guillotine." The Horseman will also film a new segment called the "Count's Head Count" where he and the Count will teach young viewers how to count to zero.

Producers additionally announced that they soon hope to bring the famous "Princess and the Pea" onto the show, but are waiting until writers figure out which letter of the alphabet she should introduce.

Pinocchio Dead at 37; Succumbs to Lengthy Battle with Dutch Elm Disease

Coke Addicts Race to Climb Old Smokey After Hearing It May Be "Covered With Snow"

Jury Says Jack Owes Sierra Club $27.1 Million

Famed beanstalk climber Jack Spencer is looking for his hen that lays golden eggs this morning, a day after being slapped with a $27.1 million judgment in favor of the Sierra Club.

Club officials sued Jack three years ago, alleging that the exotic stalk he chopped down while fleeing a giant was actually a protected endangered species. Following a three-week trial, jurors agreed, returning their multi-million dollar verdict after a mere 14 minutes of deliberation.

A club spokesman commented, "Today's ruling is not only a victory for our delicate ecosystem, but also for each and every child in this country that loves beans—all thirteen of them." The group did not announce how it plans to spend the huge financial windfall, but an anonymous source indicated that at least one club member is pumped up to try putting midgrade gas into his Toyota Prius.

Advertisement

New Book Will Revolutionize How You Play Knick Knack

Eighty-two-year-old Knick Knack World Champion Tom "This Old Man" Thomas is turning the popular game on its head with the release of a new strategy guide. Thomas promises that his book, *Rolling Home*, will reveal the secrets that helped him capture a record ten World Series of Knick Knack Knecklaces.

Thomas guarantees that readers will become better Knick Knackers once they learn his new strategic variations, including his shocking play from last year's world championship match where he *first* gave the dog a bone, *then* unleashed a double paddywhack that caught his opponent squarely in the right temple. Thomas promises to reveal even more advanced and exotic strategies, including one rumored to involve a nine-iron, a pair of pantyhose, and some mayonnaise that has already been banned in the state of Kansas.

Flat-Chested Cinderella Summons Fairy Godmother to Ask for Some Bibbity Bobbity Boobs

Beauty and the BEAST

A handsome prince gets himself into a spot of bother one night when he rudely slams his front door in the face of an old hag stuck out in a storm.

You see, it turns out this particular hag just finished a University of Phoenix course in witchcraft, and she retaliates by turning the prince into a hideous beast. She informs him that he will remain stuck as the Beast Formerly Known as Prince until he both falls in love with someone and gets someone to fall in love with him. Preferably these should be the same person.

Years pass, and things are not looking so great for Mr. Beast's quest to find a gal. His attempts to meet someone on *Love Connection* are thwarted when Chuck Woolery won't return his phone calls, and one trip to the grocery store goes particularly poorly when the cashier offers to set His Ugliness up with this cute wildebeest she knows down at the zoo.

Everything changes one fateful night when an old man gets lost in the Beast's woods and has the misfortune of thinking it would be wise to knock on the first castle door he finds. Once again, this doesn't sit too well with the Beast. (You get the feeling the Beast might have eaten an vacuum cleaner salesman or two over the years.) This time he kidnaps his trespasser and throws the man into a dungeon, where the only forms of entertainment are old issues of *Cat Fancy* magazine and the second season of *Full House* on DVD. Rough night.

Fortunately for the man, his bookworm daughter Belle manages to set down her encyclopedia long enough to show up on a brilliantly strategized rescue mission. Using skills she learned in a Dale Carnegie course, Belle schmoozes the Beast and negotiates a clever trade where she agrees to chill out at the castle for a while and/or the rest of her life, whichever comes later, in exchange for the Beast letting her pops go free. Way to play hard ball, ma'am.

Belle turns out to be quite attractive, so the Beast goes to work putting the moves on her. This includes enlisting the assistance of some singing furniture if you're relying on the Disney folk as your historical reference. Belle, of course, is not having any of th—. Wait. What? She falls for this? WTF? This plan definitely would not work for me, and I am not that ugly. Inexplicably, the next thing you know, Belle is all over the Beast like she's auditioning to pose with Fabio on the cover of a supermarket romance novel. (P.S. He still can't believe it's not butter.)

Thanks to them falling in love, the old hag's curse is broken. The Beast ceases being beastly, and let me tell you, the before-and-after pictures make those extreme makeover shows look like amateur hour. He and Belle settle in to the castle for a long and happy life together. (Admittedly, they do still have to convince a few of the transfigured staff members that "Of course you look better as a person than you did as an armoire. No, I'm not just saying that to be nice. Hey! Stop crying! Come back! I meant you used to hold a lot of junk in your trunk. Literally! Wait . . .")

the jungle book

If I have this right, a panther out wandering around in the jungle stumbles onto a basket with a baby named Mowgli in it. (I guess it is tradition in this part of the world to at least leave a nametag behind when abandoning your baby in a basket.) This is no ordinary panther, however, and he quickly realizes that the kid's best chance in life would be if he was raised by a family of wolves. Because that makes sense.

This all works out swell, at least right up until the man-eating tiger Shere Khan (not to be confused with his cousin Genghis) moves back into town. Mr. Brilliant Panther then decides that he needs to get Mowgli out of the wolf den and back to civilization, because obviously the legendary man-eating tiger would not go looking for lunch in the Man-Village or anything. Panthers . . . not exactly the brains of the animal kingdom. If you ever have to abandon your baby boy in a basket in the middle of the jungle, pray that he gets discovered by a dolphin.

Of course, having been raised by wolves and all, Mowgli has no desire to go live with people. He wants to chase little pigs and blow their houses down. He and the panther nearly have a rumble over this, and Mowgli storms off with nothing but his snazzy Superman underpants. His next stop is to move in with a big lunk of a singing bear named Baloo, who pretty much makes the panther look like Mensa material. Mowgli also at one point gets himself kidnapped by a group of monkeys and their dancing orangutan king, which makes you begin to wonder if this might collectively be the dumbest group of jungle animals in the whole freaking world.

It's only a matter of time before Shere Khan shows up as promised, and he is hungry and ready to chow down. But while he may be the jungle's number-one carnivore, old Special K turns out not to be a particularly talented weather forecaster. He makes his move for a Mowgli Meatloaf right in the middle of a thunderstorm, and lightning ends up striking a nearby tree and setting it on fire. This conveniently scares Shere Khan shitless and gets Mowgli out of Dodge unscathed.

At this point, Mowgli finally gives in and heads to the Man-Village, where, lo and behold, they have real actual living girls. And even though he may be 50% wolf, Mowgli proves to also be 100% testosterone. He eagerly checks into Man Land, where he parlays his jungle singing and dancing background into massive success as the lead singer of the new local band, the Man-Village People. (The Superman undershorts fit the role nicely.)

Rudolph's Nose No Longer Red: Credits Switch to Two-Ply Tissue

Analysts Say No Clear Favorite in Annual Dopeyest Dwarf Contest

Bunyan Opens Big and Tall Shop

When local lumberjack Paul Bunyan finally hung up his giant ax and retired last year, he knew he wouldn't be able to just sit around and stream timber sports on his iPad for long. Instead, he set out to realize a secret dream he'd had for years—opening his own Big and Tall clothing store. "When you're eighteen feet tall, you'd be amazed how hard it is to find a good looking shirt," Bunyan noted.

Though Bunyan is still debating whether to call the business "Big As Paul's" or "Big Ass Paul's," the new store is slated to open next month in the old two-story warehouse on Log Hill. (Ironically, legend has it that Log Hill was formed years ago when a young Bunyan was on a campout and took a dump in the meadow after he couldn't squeeze himself into an outhouse.)

The shop will offer every imaginable aspect of big lumberjack fashion, including flannels, Carhartts, 10-foot long suspenders, and, well, that's pretty much it. Bunyan also indicated that he hopes to add a special section of big and tall clothes for pets, allowing customers to dress their enormous blue ox in a Christmas sweater that's just as dumb looking as the one the crazy neighbor lady puts on her Chihuahua before she stuffs him into her carry-on luggage.

Goldilocks and the Three Bears

One morning, a family of bears whips up some porridge for breakfast, but goes a little overboard on the temperature. Rather than barbecue their tongues, they head off for a stroll in the woods to give everything a chance to cool down. As they are tromping through the forest, however, high drama is underway back at their house.

A golden-tressed young lass wanders up to the door, rings the bell, and waits patiently on the stoop. When nobody answers in five seconds, she whips out the crowbar stashed under her jumper and says "make way for mama."

Once inside, Goldilocks heads straight for the kitchen, finding the bears' porridge waiting in three bowls. She tries Papa Bear's bowl first, but scalds her tongue and declares that the porridge is too hot. She then samples Mama Bear's porridge, which, through a strange feat of thermodynamics, is too cold. Undeterred, Goldie then tries Baby Bear's fare, finds it to be just right, and wolfs down the entire bowl. Of course, since porridge is utterly disgusting and was only invented to be fed to children as a punishment, Goldilocks immediately barfs all over the kitchen floor. (While we're at it, anybody who thinks Little Miss Muffet was eating curds and whey by choice is nuts, too. I guarantee you that "tuffet" is just some made-up British word for "time out chair.")

With breakfast complete, Goldilocks moseys into the living room to sit down and take a load off. She plops down in Papa Bear's La-Z-Boy first, but it turns out to be too big. Mama Bear apparently got a discount on a jumbo sized recliner as well, and her chair also proves to be too large. Finally Goldilocks tries Baby Bear's seat. It ends up being just right, but Goldilocks's pleasure is short-lived when the chair collapses under her porridge-inflated weight. She makes a mental note that next time she should try breaking into a house with a treadmill.

Having now invested at least five minutes of effort into this B&E, Goldilocks is completely exhausted and ready for a nap. Her first attempt at locating a bed lands on a mattress that is too hard. She then switches from Papa to Mama Bear's bed—separate beds in this house, guess Papa Bear wasn't getting a lot of lovin'—and that turns out to be too soft. Baby Bear's bed is once again just right, and Goldilocks starts sawing logs.

The bears then come back from their walk, making the unpleasant discovery that they have been burgled. Baby Bear's stress at seeing his breakfast gone and chair obliterated only gets magnified when he discovers that Goldilocks has parked her rump on his mattress. "Someone's been sleeping in my bed, and the lady is still there!" he exclaims. Then—and here you should take a deep breath and strap yourself in for one of the most dramatic climaxes in literary history—Goldilocks wakes up and leaves the house. Story over.

Rumpelstiltskin
@RumpShaker_Gold

Tweets

Little Boy Blue @haystack29   29 min
OMG – my mom just walked in on me blowing my horn.
#neveragain

Princess Penelope @raindrenched_princess   2 h
This mattress sucks. And why does it smell like peas in here? This is definitely going on the Comment Card.
#OfCourseIAmARealPrincess

Bo Peep @LittleBoPeep11   3 h
now little bo peep has lost her jeep. searching the airport parking garage. #fml #ithastobeheresomewhere

Dan Watson @CaptainCandlestick   3 h
What the f#!@ just flew over us? Oh well, who cares... Still Rub-a-Dub-Dubbin in the tub w/ @ButcherBob99 and @BakeItBill!

Jack B. Nimble @jumper_02jbn   3 h
Just jumped over a candlestick . . . being held by some dude in a tub. #weird

Paul Bunyan @pauly_b   4 h
Danmitt! Myy funGerRs arRe toO BigG 2 teZt On thiZ Pjone! :-/

Wee Willie Winkie @TheRealWWW   5 h
Question: If your wiener turns into wood, do you go see a Hickory Dickory Doc?

Little Red Riding Hood @NorthFaceSucks_CapesRule   6 h
Just got 2 grandmas. Not gonna lie - her chin hairs have gotten really long. #gross

Captain James Hook @aarghHooker   7 h
Hope this waterbed has a warranty... #Pop #Whooooosh

Sneezy @My_Nose_Knows   8 h
Anybody got any Claritin?

Pinocchio @My_Nose_Knows_2   10 h
Judging by his schnozz, Michael Jackson must have made the opposite deal with the fairy that I did. #JustSaying #KeptGettingSmaller

facebook

Humpty Dumpty

Lord Godiva
Anybody seen my wife? Haven't seen her tonight and the horse is gone.
Like · Comment · 12 minutes ago

> **Henry Johnson** uh, duuuude... u have no idea. LOL
> 10 minutes ago Like
>
> **Boris McClintic** ur wife is hott!
> 9 minutes ago Like

Peter Peter Pumpkineater and **John Jacob Jingleheimerschmidt** are now friends.
Like · Comment · 2 hours ago ·

Judy "The Farmer's Wife" Thompson
Enough of these stupid blind mice... - at Carl's Carving Knives.
Like · Comment · 5 hours ago ·

 22 people like this.

Jack Spencer
Jack could really use some help fertilizing his Beanstalk in FarmVille!
3 hours ago via FarmVille
Comment · Like · Get some Magic Beans

Georgie Porgie
has mono.
Like · Comment · 6 hours ago ·

> **Peter Piper** Gee - wonder how that happened???
> 4 hours ago Like
>
> **The Muffin Man** Mack daddy. . .
> 3 hours ago Like

facebook

Dopey is in a relationship with **Thumbelina**.
Like · Comment · 7 hours ago ·

    6 Little People like this.

Steve Shepherd
Wolf!
Like · Comment · 9 hours ago ·

> **Brad Morrison** Shut up, Steve
> 9 hours ago   Like
>
> **Julia Gross** We're not falling for this again.
> 8 hours ago   Like
>
> **Julia Gross** What is this, like, four times now?
> 8 hours ago   Like
>
> **Steve Shepherd** No, I mean it this time. I need you're help!!!
> 8 hours ago   Like
>
> **Brad Morrison** *your, moron.
> 8 hours ago   Like
>
> **Brad Morrison** And STFU, we're sick of this.
> 8 hours ago   Like
>
> **Steve Shepherd** I'M SERIOUS! WOLF! WOLLLLLLLL—
> 8 hours ago   Like

The Hare
Race time, bitches. Kicking ass and taking naps. – with **The Tortoise**.
Like · Comment · 11 hours ago ·

    Rip Van Winkle likes this.

Goldilocks is attending Break-In at the Bears' House.
Like · Comment · 13 hours ago ·

facebook

Emperor Randy Caesar
Just outfitted the palace with a new arse-washing device called a "bidet."
Like · Comment · 14 hours ago ·

> **Maynard Fanduno** That sounds awesome. Where'd you get it?
> 10 hours ago Like
>
> **Emperor Randy Caesar** It's from France.
> 10 hours ago Like
>
> **Maynard Fanduno** Of course – the country of ass-wipes too lazy to wipe their own asses.
> 9 hours ago Like

Old McDonald
You'll never guess what I found in my wife's closet...
Like · Comment · 15 hours ago ·

> **Jack Sprat** A muu muu here and a muu muu there?
> 13 hours ago Like

Prince Charming is in an open relationship with **Cinderella** and **Snow White** and **Sleeping Beauty** and **Oprah**.
Like · Comment · 16 hours ago ·

> **The Big Bad Wolf** Get some...
> 9 hours ago Like

About the Author - Topher Goggin

After retiring at age nine from a brief career in magic-where he performed as "The Great Tophini" and once made a death-defying escape from being tied to a toilet-Topher Goggin has served as "editor" of a childhood sports newspaper with 50 non-paying subscribers, hosted a college radio show that pulled in as many as 30 listeners thanks to giving away over $4000 in prizes, and unwittingly instigated a local controversy when he accidentally convinced his hometown that a nuclear waste dump was on the way in an April Fools' Day newspaper article. He currently works as Mr. Small Town Lawyer, kind of like "Ed" on that old show on NBC, except that his office isn't in a bowling alley. He also engages in traditional lawyerly activities like teaching junior golf and announcing high school football and basketball on the radio. He lives in Alma, Michigan.

About the Illustrator - Rick Cunningham

Owner of Cunninghams, an award-winning design/illustration studio specializing in marketing support services, Rick has been seriously devoting more time to fun projects (like this book). His bold style gets right to the point with clear visual expression. He brings a wealth of experience on accounts as big as General Motors and as small as his brother's restaurant. Rick also taught commercial art at Lansing Community College. He lives in Lansing, Michigan.

Acknowledgments/Dedications

This book is dedicated to my grandmother, Gretchen Goggin, the person who first inspired me to write and served as my initial typist and editor when I was little. She would have acted completely mortified if she read this thing, but I'm pretty sure she would have secretly loved it.

I owe a big thank you to my mom for coming up with the name "Not Your Mother's Goose." After all, despite entries being open to the entire extended family (including my parents' dogs), the only things anyone else came up with were craptastic ideas like "Let Sleeping Frogs Lie" or "Once Upon a Mime." Ding. My sister also said she'd never speak to me again if I didn't put her name in here somewhere, so . . . Stephanie Goggin. Done.

Thank you as well to everyone who provided input along the way, most importantly my ninth grade English teacher, Mary Jane Kooiman. Let's just hope this is better than my "bird motif newspaper" about *To Kill a Mockingbird*.

I similarly need to thank Rick Cunningham for his amazing work on the illustrations you've just seen. They are incredible. He also deserves some sort of award for putting up with me and my roughly eight gazillion suggestions and revisions throughout the layout process. Rick, I hope your Fairy Godmother and/or Oprah brings you that Osterizer you've always wanted ASAP.

Copyright © 2015, 2018 by Topher Goggin
All rights reserved.

Published in the United States of America by
CRD Press, PO Box 488, Alma, MI 48801

www.notyourmothersgoose.com

Design by Rick Cunningham and Topher Goggin

ISBN-10: 099096440X
ISBN-13: 978-0-9909644-0-7

www.ingramcontent.com/pod-product-compliance
Lightning Source LLC
Chambersburg PA
CBHW080229020526
44113CB00051B/2632